Fathers

Fathers

music by
Kurt Bestor

text by
Brett Walker

photographs by
Jon Moe

BOOKCRAFT
Salt Lake City, Utah

Library of Congress Catalog Card Number: 98-72342
ISBN 1-57008-440-8

First Printing, 1998

Printed in the United States of America

To the man who I once told I never wanted to be like but now find myself enjoying our similarities more and more every day. You're the dad of a lifetime, the father every boy I know wishes he had.

And to my grandfathers, for teaching me how to play "You Are My Sunshine" and other nameless songs on the harmonica (and never playing them the same way twice), making me ticklish, and calling me "mister."

To Marvin, who was the kind of man that makes everyone who knew him hug my wife when they find out she is his daughter. Thanks for giving me the "Spearmint Girl With The Wrigley Eyes" (e. e. cummings).

Finally, to my Heavenly Father, for guiding the pen in my hand and all else.

ACKNOWLEDGMENTS

Seeing our day, the ancient prophet Malachi spoke of a turning of "the heart of the fathers to the children, and the heart of the children to their fathers" (Malachi 4:6). Fathers play a key role in the happiness and success of the family. In some cases that father figure must, by circumstance, be supplanted by a grandfather, uncle, cherished friend, or church leader. Still, fathers are essential to every family.

Families Worldwide is a nonprofit organization focused on strengthening families throughout the world. Its value-based programs are doing much to turn the hearts of fathers back to their children, strengthening that special bond that binds our families, communities, nations, and our world.

Families Worldwide is pleased to co-sponsor this wonderful tribute to fathers. If you would like to find out how this organization can help your family, or if you would like to be a part of this important effort, please call 801-562-6178 or visit our Web site at http://www.fww.org

FOREWORD

I wish that I could take credit for the genesis of this project. That honor, how-ever, belongs to a group of sons who, like me, pay homage to their respective fathers and who struggle daily to live up to their standards: Lon Hendersen, Tim Doot, Brad Pelo, and Brett Walker. From my humble vantage point, these fellow collaborators have raised the fatherhood standard.

The composers and lyricists of the musical material also approached their task with a sincerity and dedication that's rare in recorded music today. Their oft times very personal approach to the songs has added tremendous depth and emotion to the beautiful photography and written word.

Our hope for this project is to celebrate the best of the institution of fatherhood, to rekindle the love between father and child, and to draw closer to the Father of us all.

—KURT BESTOR

Photograph by Doug Martin

INTRODUCTION

Much has been said about men as fathers. For better or for worse, father literature either builds them up as movers of the earth or tears them down as rascals. For me, the journey began like all others and has brought me to a point. A point peppered with overwhelming love for my children, mixed with a desire to see them perfected. One of wonderment about whether I will ever match my wife as a parent-*extraordinaire*. One with night dreams of my own grandfather's impending death. One of a sense of insufficiency about my relationship with my dad.

In ways, I feel unable to write. In others, I feel as qualified as any "fatherson" to jot down thoughts and attempt somehow to weave prose, both simple and compelling, about men as fathers. Like any fatherson, I am only flesh and memories, none of which may apply to anyone else's experience with this subject.

Men as fathers. Fathers as men. The people who make them so—sons, daughters, "wifemothers."

Men as fathers. We all have one. Natural, grand, in-laws, and figures. My old man, yours, the boss, someone unknown, the head of the house, the silhouette in the doorway. They are all lawn-mowing, whisker-burning, newspaper-reading, garbage-disposing, back-rubbing, car-fixing, love-handles-and-all "Dad."

Universal and constant in name, the role is as elusive as a brook trout on a spring day or a hole-in-one on any other.

Rock-a-bye, baby, sweet baby.

He gave me the breath of life.

"What time should we wake our baby in the mornings?"
"Which is the front and which is the back of this diaper?"
New fathers naively ask questions that hint at the life-altering impact of a baby's arrival—an event that cannot be absorbed in a moment. A new father and the new baby he holds are alike in many ways: a full lifetime lies ahead to grow and learn, to become. More than mothers, fathers mimic the ways of babies—not knowing much and quickly forgetting the way things are supposed to be:

Questions. Questions repeated throughout the child's life as the man continually reshapes himself as a father.

Feelings. Feelings that science can't describe. Thinking, *I want to put you in my pocket and take you to work with me.*

Promises. Promises made in the dark hours of night when no other sound is heard. Whispering, "I will always love you. I will teach you to pray. I will never do anything to harm you. I will send you to the best college. I will let you take dance lessons."

Becoming. Becoming at each passing stage a father once more—like a bridge over a river under which the water is constantly and rapidly changing. Baby, toddler, adolescent, teen, young adult, adult, peer—at each point a new father.

From one father we draw our breath.
Again and again.
(*Genesis 2:7.*)

Infancy conforms to nobody;

all conform to it; so that one babe

commonly makes four or five out of

the adults who prattle and play to it.

—RALPH WALDO EMERSON

I love little
children, and it
is not a slight
thing when they,
who are fresh
from God,
love us.
—Charles Dickens

men becoming fathers

And he shall be like a tree planted by the rivers of water. —*Psalm 1:3*

The measure of a man can be taken quickly in simple circumstances—when standing with him under a park building at a rainy youth soccer game. In that short time you can know whether this is a man full of himself or full of others.

If full of himself he will talk about his endeavors, hobbies, and job. Five minutes will pass slowly.

If full of others his words will clearly reveal so.

I met such a man. He asked most of the questions. His comments were peppered with "we" and "us"—referring to the people that made him "be." He reflected on my words and talked about his children, his wife, his parents, his grandfather. He referred to these people as important members of his community, not just a network that he used when he needed one. His was the language of the blessed, semi-divine.

He commented on how nice it was to have nothing to do for a minute while the rain poured. I was impressed that he stood clean from the sludge of the world, almost as if he didn't know that it existed. He made me feel at peace. This rain was good for me.

Five minutes was all it took.

As the rain stopped he looked me in the eye, shook my hand, and thanked me for the chat, commenting on how clean the earth looked now. I wondered what block this guy was chipped off from, or if he wasn't the old block himself.

I knew I had just met a father.

The make of a man is best defined not by what he thinks about when he's made or paid to think, but what he thinks about when he doesn't have to think at all.

fathers

as

men

Friendship is a sheltering tree. —*Samuel Taylor Coleridge*

From a wife:

"My daughters always kid me that they wish he wasn't taken. I say, 'I saw him first.'

"Driving to the store one day, somewhere between spring and fall, I felt like grabbing a mug of chocolate and pretending it was morning. I wanted to waltz slowly into his den, careful not to tease the hardwood floor into squeaking, and rub his shoulders. This would distract him, I was sure, but the chocolate was for him—he needed a distraction! I'd kiss his ear and rub his arm. He'd softly say in bewildered tones, 'What? I'm busy.' But I'd persist until he drank the chocolate and curled me into his embrace . . .

"I nearly hit a pedestrian.

"But he's my children's father, he's my best friend. Our friendship is the highest form of collaboration.

"I've never heard him say, 'Me first.' But he always goes first—into the dark kitchen to get a drink for a child at night, to cross a stream on a wobbly log and test it for the rest of us, or into the water to check the temperature.

"He's a good man. He gets busy at work but never lost. He has harsh words for people who don't play fair. He brings me flowers. He talks more about sportsmanship than a ref's bad call. His touch is always friendly, his grip only for his golf clubs. He prays with me.

"He gives me consideration for my feelings, almost a payment on a loan without ever acting like he's being overcharged.

"Of course he has other 'women'—a car, a boat, a fishing rod, and projects around the house—all that he calls she. 'Let's get her done. Listen to her roar. She'll take a pint of oil and that'll be plenty.'

"And when the kids are down, when we're alone, I feel like I am home."

My fair one, let us swear an eternal friendship.

—MOLIÈRE

fathers as husbands

Train up a child in the way he should go: and when he is old, he will not depart from it.

—Proverbs 22:6

Glimpses. Fathers get only occasional glimpses of whether or not it's working. *You think I'm being too hard on you? You want more freedom? You want to play three sports at the same time? You want to sing in a rock band? You want to know the purpose of life?*

Glimpses—things occasionally provided to fathers—while the rest of the world holds them in full view:

A young . . . soldier in World War II . . . wore both a standard wristwatch and an older, larger pocket watch. His buddies noticed him regularly looking at both watches, and asked why he checked the time twice.

"The wristwatch tells me the time here where we are, but the big watch Pa gave me tells me the time it is in Utah," said the soldier. "When the big watch says 5:00 A.M., I know dad is rolling out to milk the cows. And any night when it says 7:30, I know the whole family is around the well-spread table on their knees thanking the Lord for what's on the table and asking him to watch over me and keep me clean and honorable. It's those things that make me want to fight when the going gets tough," said the young man. "I can find out what time it is here easy enough. What I want to know is what time it is in Utah." (Richard Nash, *Lengthen Your Smile* [Salt Lake City: Deseret Book, 1996], p. 153.)

Train up. Teach them your values and then some. Show them the path that you wished you had walked as a youth. Help them know the Savior, even if only to know him better yourself.

Great fires are built from very small kindling. Start one now, and bask in its warmth and light when you are old.

I would rather have you know me merely as the result of one of my father's earlier experiments.

—CHARLES EDISON,
SON OF THOMAS EDISON

My heart belongs to Daddy. —*Cole Porter*

Kids are awesome. Mine color my life like a rainbow. One day, in the middle of an important meeting with my boss's boss, my cellular phone went off. "Dad! Mom just won a sweepstakes in the mail!"

"Wow," I said, smiling at those around the table who were staring at the word as it left my mouth.

"Yeah. She's not here right now, but if she's one of the first fifty people to call in, she could win even more!"

"Wow," was all I could think to say again. "What sweepstakes is this that she won?"

"*Field and Stream.*"

"*Hmmm.* You tell her the minute that she gets home to call in immediately to be one of the first fifty people." We hung up. Everyone around the table chuckled as we contrasted our adult skepticism with my son's youthful naiveté.

Adults tell all sorts of stories about their offspring—stories that at the time they occurred were not funny at all but in time became humorous.

Bill Cosby tells of being talked into feeding his children chocolate cake for breakfast while his wife slept peacefully upstairs. "I thought about the ingredients in chocolate cake: milk and eggs and wheat, all part of good nutrition.

"So there my five children sat, merrily eating chocolate cake for breakfast, occasionally stopping to sing: *Dad is the greatest dad you can make! For breakfast he gives us chocolate cake!*

"The party lasted until my wife appeared, staggered slightly, and said, 'Chocolate cake for *breakfast*? Where did you all get *that?*'

"'*He* gave it to us! *He* made us eat it!,' said my five adorable ingrates in one voice; and then my eight-year-old added, '*We* wanted eggs and cereal.'" (Bill Cosby, *Fatherhood*, [New York: Doubleday & Company, Inc., 1986], pp. 58–59.)

On an equally colorful day, I was sitting by another son in church, pondering life and my personal progress. He leaned over and whispered, "Dad, why do pilots say 'mayonnaise' when they are in danger?"

I said, "*May Day*, they say *May Day.*"

May your own life be filled with sweepstakes, chocolate cake, and mayonnaise.

William Haddad was an associate of Kennedy's. After JFK was assassinated, his young son John asked Mr. Haddad, "Are you a daddy?" Haddad admitted that he was. Said little John, "Then will you throw me up in the air?"

And then Emma saw the biggest, softest, cuddliest thing she had ever seen. It was her father! "Will you be my pet?" she asked. "Always," said her father. (David McPhail, Emma's Pet, New York: Scholastic, 1985.)

daddy

We went camping, just me and my dad.
Dad drove the car because I'm too little. —*Mercer Mayer*

It seems that everyone learns to enjoy the outdoors, even if only a little, from the men in their lives.

> When I was five he taught me to fish. We walked to a pond filled with bluegill and sun perch. He hooked a worm on my line, sat beside me waiting for a hit, and then he helped me take the fish off the hook. He untangled line, chased away snakes and picked off the ticks I acquired en route to the pond. We could sit all afternoon along the bank, listening to frogs, watching turtles and filling a gunnysack with keepers. (Mary Pipher, *Reviving Ophelia* [Ballantine Books, 1994] p. 115.)

With my own boys there were always plenty of keepers, usually on the smaller side, until we decided that we really didn't like the taste of fish so much. So we switched to catch-and-release. We could still fish together and not have to make a meal of it.

It was from my grandfather on my mom's side, though, that I learned how to use my eyes to see the world around me. My grandfather taught me that the world existed for me to build a better one. "This land," he would say, extending his arm, "was once all sagebrush and more rocks than I'd like to remember." It was now a fertile field with three cuttings of alfalfa a year.

He would let nature provide the example and then comment on what I should be learning. "Goodness," he would have said, "flows like a river; the deeper it is, the less noise it makes." When I was sad or discouraged, he would say, "Wild things don't get sad. Only people do. Listen to the birds. Do they sound sad?" And, "There is nowhere better than nature to witness the majesty of God."

He'd spent his life as a farmer, learning an encyclopedia of lessons from the earth.

He left me with a few parting comments: "Go after your dreams. Listen carefully to the lessons being taught by the trees and rocks. Remember the same fear that makes you run away from something can turn you back to stare at what it was that made you run away. So rather than run, just stare it in the face until the fear goes away."

The eyes of my eyes are opened. —e. e. cummings

Nature always wears the colors of the spirit.
—RALPH WALDO EMERSON

I'll be my father's son forever.

When I was young I thought I would never please him. I never quite understood him. He would sit knee-to-knee with other young men but always seemed so distant from me, so busy. Maybe *I* was just inaccessible.

Somehow we gradually built a wall that has taken me years just to see over and only partially tear down. The good news is that I can hear a pickax chipping away on his side too.

It seems that I can now see into his heart—if only a little—and he seems very satisfied with me. Even though we chose completely different directions in life. Even though I'm in a high-tech profession and he was always in a high-touch business. In spite of all of this, I think I've learned that he's my dad—and I'm his son.

He writes! I never knew that. Just the other day, I found this:

Here comes some hail—It didn't snow
And now the wind is starting to blow.
We're out of wood, the oil's spent,
We'll be glad when this winter's went.

We have more in common than merely matching noses. We both love the early morning hours—a time for meditation and prayer. We can probably be found gazing at the same stars on more nights than either of us realizes. Neither of us ever asks for directions. We're now both fathers and sons. I like my middle name (my father's given name) better all of the time.

Shakespeare said, "'Tis a happy thing to be the father unto many sons" (King Henry the Sixth, Part III). Well, it's a very happy thing to be the son of a father like mine.

Under a spreading chestnut tree
The village smithy stands;
The smith a mighty man is he,
With large and sinewy hands;
And the muscles of his brawny arms
Are strong as iron bands.

—HENRY WADSWORTH LONGFELLOW

The figure in the doorway —*Robert Frost*

I have never heard of a man who on his deathbed said he wished that he had spent more time at the office. The tough thing is that in today's busy world time has to be spent at the office—more time than I'd like. My kids often see me only in the dark. They know me by my silhouette in the doorway at bedtime. I vow every day to spend more time with them—it would be good for us all.

On a recent drive home to pack my bag for a short trip to another city, I called my little girl. I hadn't seen her that morning and now wouldn't for a few days. She said as I neared the house, "Dad, can I just talk with you until your car comes around the corner?" Even on a cellular phone that kind of conversation is priceless.

I'm trying to owe less all the time and dig out from under this pressure. Someday I'd like to get back to a relaxing job—one that my kids will understand and be proud of. Now they think I work in an office and have meetings. Everything else is a blur.

I still want to be Super Dad, and be there for my kids, my wife, and myself. I'm trying to remember that even though I go to work in the day and fight like a lion for my prey, that when I come home I must put fighting ways aside and nurture and care for my cubs. My dream is that one of them will appear on TV someday, and instead of the usual "Hi, Mom!" they'll say "Hi, Dad!" I'm relying on a power greater than my own to get there.

Still, I sometimes feel like I'm watching them grow up in pictures, or that I only know how tall they are by the measure of how they fill their beds at night. I'd like it to be different. I hope they know this too.

Bye baby bunting,

Daddy's gone a-hunting.

Gone to get a rabbit skin

To wrap the baby bunting in.

As I start the twilight years of my life, I try to look back and figure out what it was all about. I'm still not sure what is meant by good fortune and success. I know fame and power are for the birds. But then suddenly life comes into focus for me. And, ah, there stand my kids. I love them.

—LEE IACOCCA

You can't run away from trouble. There ain't no place that far. —*Uncle Remus, from Splash Mountain at Disneyland*

Fatherhood requires flexible shoulders. Shoulders to carry children that have lost all energy in their legs after walking around the mall for just a few minutes. Shoulders to shrug when a toddler is sitting in a pile of unraveled video tape, personally inspecting each inch of "The Sound of Music." Shoulders to hold when your boy calls from school and says, "Dad, guess who just got kicked out of college?"

Shoulders to put to the wheel of fatherhood each day, leaning in with all your force to budge and nudge a rock that never noticeably moves.

As a boy I found an old lawn mower in a field. What a find! My dad said I could bring it home. I cleaned it up, checked the oil, and put some gas in. It wouldn't start. I took the spark plug out, removed the starting mechanism, and made adjustments. I pulled and pulled and pulled. Finally I got a spark, and it started. What a celebration I had: this, my baby, was working like it should, a well-behaved lawn mower.

So, how is fathering done? Day-by-day? Where are the spark plugs? Where's the starter? Does anyone have a simple plan for starting a child? For my child?

It seems like nothing but a child can start so small and end so big. Or cost so much. Or catch you so unprepared. Or require so much cleanup. Or take as much soul-searching to reconcile.

How many milk shakes will you drink together, trying to see eye-to-eye over your straws and spoons? View it as generating demand for milk products. Think of all the dairy farmers you keep in business.

Just like the lawn mower, you pull and you pull and you pull, you brush off the leaves, clean the spark plug, change the oil, and give it another try. You believe in sparks. You have faith in sparks. You pray for sparks. You see sparks in your sleep.

Someday there will be a spark. And it will take off on its own.

A GOOD TRAINER CAN HEAR A HORSE SPEAK TO HIM. A GREAT TRAINER CAN HEAR HIM WHISPER.
—MONTY ROBERTS

Your son at five is your master,
at ten your slave, at fifteen
your double, and after that,
your friend or your foe,
depending on his bringing up.

—HASDAI IBN SHAPRUT

Doing is always more effective than talking.

Am I doing or talking? I look back on the times my younger children have asked me to play: "Dad, can I ask you a question? Maybe it's a *no* answer, but would you catch a couple pitches?" How many times have I said no in so many words? How long will they keep asking?

So, I've set out to make a difference. Instead of perfecting my lecturing skills this year, I'm going to walk the walk. I'll learn to throw a ball better. I'll figure out the rules to soccer so that I can participate intelligently. I'll enjoy saxophone solos and piano duets. I'll choreograph dances so that my daughter will think I'm the best dancer around. I'll purchase a fishing license—my son and I will learn to think like fish together. Yes, I will.

I'd rather see a sermon than hear one any day;
I'd rather one should walk with me than merely point the way.
The eye's a better pupil and more willing than the ear,
Fine counsel is confusing, but example's always clear;
And the best of all the preachers are the men who live their creeds,
For to see good put in action is what everybody needs.

I soon can learn to do it if you'll let me see it done;
I can watch your hands in action, but your tongue too fast may run.
And the lecture you deliver may be very wise and true,
But I'd rather get my lessons by observing what you do;
For I might misunderstand you and the high advice you give,
But there's no misunderstanding how you act and how you live.

— *Edgar A. Guest, 1881*

I'm determined to be a father of action! I'm determined to *do* more than I *talk*. I will teach my children to walk by holding out my hands to catch them. I will run alongside their bikes as they overcome their fears of crashing and gain confidence on two wheels. I will cheer louder than other parents at sporting events.

And my lecturing skills will go dormant or maybe disappear altogether. I will never be too busy, or at least I'll wake up earlier to get busy stuff out of the way. I will say *yes* and *yes* again. I will.

A MAN OF WORDS

When I rest

AND NOT OF DEEDS

BE A VERB

IS LIKE A GARDEN

I rust.

FULL OF WEEDS.

If the root be holy, so are the branches. —*Romans 11:16*

At my wife's family gatherings, it's clear where they all came from: Grandpa, old and feeble.

Grandma will laugh as she tells stories about him—about how whenever they drive together, she can squeeze his knee as a signal to slow down or to be careful or to notice something.

She tells how a few years ago for their twenty-fifth wedding anniversary he said to all who had gathered, "You didn't need to come all this way. Your presents were enough," meaning the other kind of *presence*. The family always chuckles when Grandma recalls how once in church he'd fallen asleep. A choir was singing "How Great Thou Art," and she poked him to wake up and listen. Coming to, Grandpa thought it was the closing congregational hymn and started singing along quietly. She poked him again—to be quiet—but he sang louder, if only for a moment, until he realized that everyone's eyes were pointed you-know-where. Grandma always wipes her eyes at the end of these stories.

We like to laugh at him. He's the funniest guy we know. He obviously doesn't intend to be so funny but he makes us realize why we are the way we are. And we probably laugh a little because he's perfect in so many ways—a finely honed knife after a lifetime of constant use.

He's filled with good advice on how to view life: "There's a miracle a day if only you look for it." On overcoming challenges: "Put your mind to it and you'll get it done. Give it a little time, and things will work out." On what you say: "I've never used profanity and don't have much use for a man that does." On working with others: "People are about as good as you expect them to be." On everything else: "Cats alive!"

At night, when the grandchildren are sick or filled with bad dreams, he takes them to the kitchen for a drink of water. He stands there, hair unkempt, night-breath and all, and tells them that they'll feel better in a minute. It always seems to work. Why don't more doctors prescribe a drink of water?

We like to poke at the veins on the back of his hands, poofy and inflated. I'd like veins like that someday. Every one of us would. Are there exercises to make us be like him?

Thanks, Grandpa.

Everyone has at least
one sermon in him.
—saying

I've never been a father before.

Somehow every day I feel like I've never done this before—been a father, you know. I feel completely prepared for yesterday but have no idea of what may happen tomorrow. At least not with kids this age, in these new situations (why didn't anyone tell me?), in my circumstances, at my age, and knowing what I know now.

My heart often pleads with my head. My head pleads with Him above.

Dear Father in Heaven,

I'm not sure how to ask this—but please help me be the best I can.

Lead me in a more excellent way. Be my burning and shining light to guide me as I father my young.

Do not leave me alone. Help me to walk in the light of your fire and not that of my own making. Please make my arms strong in doing your work. May my soul delight more in my children than in the things of this world.

Fill my wife with strength for our kids and patience for me. Help us grow together and lead our team to victory. Fill her face with happiness and deliver her from gray hairs.

Help us to show our children how to resolve conflict peacefully, how to live moderately and appropriately, and how to abide by the same standards that we lay out for them. Help us teach them that adulthood is not a destination but just another stage in life. Help us to teach them about you.

Help me to know how to braid my daughter's hair when my wife is out of town.

Oh, and lift up my children—spare them from tragedy. Don't let my eyes water my pillow. Help me understand the tugging in their heads and the tumult in their hearts.

Help me to help them. Help me to whisper. Help me to develop a gentle touch.

Help my children know that many of my dreams are put aside for them. That I live for them. That I wear yesterday's clothes so that they can dress in today's.

I became a father when I didn't know any better. And now that I do, I would move the world to do it again.

This is my life. I am father.

Amen.

A great man is he who has not lost the heart of a child.
—Mencius

Am I drawing closer,
    nearer my God to thee?
Or is this ethereal feeling
    coming from the sights I see?
I walk the road alone
    yet guided by thy grace
When I look closer, no closer still,
    I always see thy face.

Father's Lullaby

Music and lyrics by Kurt Bestor

Oh, rock-a-bye, Sweet Baby, in the treetop.
When threat'ning winds blow the cradle will rock.
But when the bough breaks, and the cradle does fall
Know this, my little one,
Trust me, my precious son,
I'll catch you, cradle and all.

Soon all the king's horses will take you away
And into the battle to fight for the day.
But when in the moments of doubt and of fear,
Know this, my noble son,
Always, my special one,
I'll catch you, cradle and all.

So, slumber
All the night through.
Peace abide.
Don't hurry, tomorrow
    will come too soon.

As twilight approaches a
    star   becomes dim,
And father to son, as he
    fades, calls to him.
"The bough is now
    breaking, and I'm soon
    to fall.
Would you, my caring son,
Now that my life is done,
Please catch me, cradle and all?"

Vocals: Kenneth Cope
Piano/Synth: Kurt Bestor
Cello: Ellen Bridger

He'll Take Me Home

Music by Kurt Bestor
Lyrics by Brett Walker
(Additional lyrics by Kurt Bestor)

If rough hands can still touch softly,
If they bend to lift the child,
Then his arms, so strong from bearing all . . .
Holding you. Holding me.
A home for the refugee.

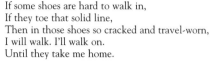

If some shoes are hard to walk in,
If they toe that solid line,
Then in those shoes so cracked and travel-worn,
I will walk. I'll walk on.
Until they take me home.

Even if the world confronts
This old man.
Measure twice, cut once,
My old man.
This man in front of me,
Is all the man I need to see.
He's the man I want to be.
He'll take me home. He'll take me home.

Even though no hands can lift a falling world,
No shoes can walk with every soul,
Still he walks with me.
His voice has never reached above the crowd.
So lovingly he turned about
And looked back to me.

If any voice can move the world,
But whisper still in one child's ear,
Then breathlessly I'll run to heed the call.
I will come. I'll still come.

If failing eyes can still remember,
When they saw a life ahead,
Then through his wrinkled eyes I'll see,
Seeing through, see into,
The man I want to be.

Even if the world confronts
This old man.
Measure twice, cut once,
My old man.
This man in front of me,
Is all the man I need to see.
He's the man I want to be.
He'll take me home. He'll take me home.

Rough hands.
Worn shoes.
Tired voice.
Those eyes.

Vocals: John McVey
Piano/Accordian/Synth: Kurt Bestor
Fiddle: Kelly Parkinson
Cello: Ellen Bridger

Two Roads

Music and lyrics by Kurt Bestor

Two roads, two separate paths
Meet at the crossway, and pausing to contemplate
If two roads could ever lead to
Places unshown and faces unknown,
To two.

And then on that sacred day
Two became one, and twice is the joy they find
In traveling that single road
That through all the storms and the rain-filled days
Still rises above to a better place . . . of joy.

Theirs is the true measure of love
That they believe no one so loved
Before or will again.
They have found the true treasure of love
In quiet vows and promises
Whispered long ago
When two roads turned into one.

Oh, sunny day
Come light the way . . . the way.
Our way.

Long has the journey been.
Hard is the road.
But gone is the resting place.
For after that final turn,
Ahead, in the light of another day
Is road after road leading to a place . . . of joy.

Theirs is the true measure of love
That they believe no one so loved
Before or will again.
They have found the true treasure of love
In quiet vows and promises
Whispered long ago
When two roads turned into one.

> *This is the true season of love, when we*
> *believe that we alone can love, that no one*
> *could ever have loved so before us, and that*
> *no one will ever love in the same way after us.*
> *—Johann Wolfgang von Goethe*

Vocals: Dave Barrus
Piano: Kurt Bestor

What He Means

Music and lyrics by John McVey

He said, "You've got to learn to wait,
'Cause often things you want come slow."
He said, "You've got to learn to try,
'Cause if you don't you'll never know."
He said, "Learn this as a young man,
Make it part of your routine,
And it'll save some trouble later."
Now I know what he means.

There were times when he would scold me,
Times he was much less than polite.
It made me doubt all that he told me,
The more he said that he was right.
He said someday I'd understand it,
When I had seen all he had seen.
I'd become too cool to listen.
But now I know what he means.

Now I know that the language of affection
Is sometimes harshly spoken.
Now I know that part of loving someone
Is you must watch their hearts be broken.

Until I caught myself repeating,
The things he'd told me in my youth,
Could I get past my own resentment,
And begin to see the truth,
That I'd expected his perfection,
So that I might have my own.
And that's the thing that came between us
But now I know what he means . . . to me.
Now I know what he means.

Vocals: John McVey
Hammond B3: Sam Cardon

The Greatest of Them All
Music and lyrics by Kurt Bestor

Sitting back in history,
The old school marm's got it wrong you see.
She's got Longfellow, Lincoln, and Liszt on the
    ol' chalkboard.

But before you flunk her little quiz,
Let me learn ya the way that it really is.
There's only one answer no matter the question.
Only one man, sir, when greatness is mentioned.
As luck would have it he's livin' right here . . .
With my mom.

He can "EmC-square" like Einstein,
Swat a ball like DiMaggio.
And according to Mom, he's still turning heads,
Like Valentino-oooh yeah!
He's got it all figured out like Edison,
Even the clock on the VCR!
If they gave out a Nobel Prize for Dads,
It's his by far!

With language inspired by Shakespeare,
And a hook shot like Doctor J's,
"Oh, where for art thou, charging foul?
He was hammered on that play!!"
He's as muscular as Superman.
But you'll never see him in those tights.
When they pass out the Oscar for Dads,
His name's in lights!

Like good ol' George & his cherry tree,
When the question's asked of me,
I cannot tell a lie.
Who is the greatest of them all,
With his picture on the wall,
My wall of fame . . .

It's been awhile since that history test—
30 years give or take a day.
And here I sit with my loving wife and a dog.

When out on the street my 2.5 kids,
Are tellin' their friends just how it is.
And to my surprise when they're asked who's
    the greatest,
They stand up real proud and without hesitatin'.
If you listen real close you can hear them sayin' . . .

He can "EmC-square" like Einstein,
Swat a ball like DiMaggio.
And according to Mom, he's still turning heads,
Like Valentino-oooh yeah!
He's got it all figured out like Edison,
Even the clock on the VCR!

He drives a bit like Andretti
In his Oldsmobile racin' car.

With language inspired by Shakespeare,
And a hook shot like Doctor J,
"Oh, where for art thou, charging foul?
He was hammered on that play!!"
He's as muscular as Superman,
But you'll never see him in those tights.
He runs the house a bit like Reagan,
But not quite so far to the right.

Vocals: John McVey
Backup Vocals: Holli Ammon and Tonya Terry
Piano/Trumpet: Kurt Bestor

Hold on to This
Music by Kurt Bestor & Felicia Sorensen
Lyrics by Felicia Sorensen
Arranged and produced by Todd Sorensen

Let's go running like we used to do.
Let's run far away from the pain that chases you.

We could go down the river, drifting to memories
That carry us to a better day.

Chorus
I'm gonna hold on to this,
Hold on to you.
And I'll be there for you
To hold on to.
Even when the best of times
Have passed us by,
I'm gonna hold on to this.

Let's go reeling, spinning awhile,
In another world where everything's benign.

And love is never ending, leading the way
To a better time without good-byes.

Chorus

I'm not gonna think about
Anywhere we didn't go.
I'm just gonna lean
On the love that we've known.

Chorus

Vocals: Felicia Sorensen
Piano: Vince Frates
Guitar: Michael Dowdle

More Than Just a Name

Music by Kurt Bestor
Lyrics by Brett Walker and Kurt Bestor

As a babe he held me deep inside his rugged arms,
Then later on he tossed a ball to me.
Playing "one-on-one" between dusk and dawn
I thought that's all my father had for me.

Once a willful youth I told him who I was,
That I was not like him nor meant to be.
I wanted a chapter to call my own,
So I tried to take my father out of me.

I just tried to take my father out.
I just reached on in and pulled the inside out.
I just tried to take my father out.
Then looked within.

One morning as I pulled myself up out of bed,
And searched the mirror for the man I knew,
There through the sleep and the morning fog,
His face searched back at me in odd review.

Many winding roads and a thousand tales
Etched into a face strangely the same.
From curious eyes to that crooked smile,
He's a part of me in more than just the name.

I just tried to take my father out.
I just reached on in and pulled the inside out.
I just tried to take my father out.
Then looked within.
I missed all that's him.

It's not just a chance act of nature,
Explained by a chart or the stars
Traveling from his father's father to this father's son.

Now my own two sons, they have me seeing clear,
How I have grown in them and they in me.
In spite of the changes the world rearranges,
You can't take a father out.
I won't let my father out.
You can't take my father out . . . of me.

Vocals: Peter Breinholt
Backup Vocals: Nancy Hanson
Piano: Kurt Bestor

Show Me the Way

Music by Sam Cardon
Lyrics by Don Stirling
(Additional music and lyrics by Kurt Bestor and John McVey)

I tiptoe through the kitchen,
And make my way upstairs.
A wall of pictures scolds me silently
As another midnight passes.
With the children fast asleep.
I find the note my son has left for me.

Be there for me, I'm here for you,
Show me the way, and I'll follow through.
Lift me up slowly, when it's too hard to stand,
You are my hero, my best pal, my dad.

In a flash it's now me looking
Out the window by the couch,
Still hoping for the Buick to appear.
He promised to be home tonight,
And the time would just be ours.
But soon the waiting hours turn to tears.

Be there for me, I'm here for you,
Show me the way, and I'll follow through.
Lift me up slowly, when it's too hard to stand,
You are my hero, my best pal, my dad.

He was the shadow in the doorway
In the middle of the night.
He would stand there for a minute, then be gone.
Now I'm standing in the same place
That he stood all those years
Casting that same shadow.

Tonight it's one more airplane,
One more disappearing act,
A promise to be home left undone.
But tonight somewhere there's laughter
And a tender, warm embrace,
Shared between a father and a son.

Be there for me, I'm here for you,
Show me the way, and I'll follow through.
Lift me up slowly, when it's too hard to stand,
You are my hero, my best pal, my dad.

Vocals: John McVey
Synth: Kurt Bestor

You Can't Run Away from Trouble

Music and lyrics by Moses Hogan

Think of us and the love we share,
It would be hard to make it alone.
The problems of life may seem unfair.
You know they come to make us strong.

We've got to have faith in all of our endeavors,
No matter how great or small.
But when trouble comes, we must face the task.
Running away is not the answer.

You can't run away from trouble.
There ain't no place that far.
You better find out what road to walk,
If you're gonna be with us at all.
You've got to face it, then you'll make it,
When our problems seem so very hard.
You can't run away from trouble.
There ain't no place that far.

Stand for what you know is right,
No matter what your friends may say.
In you I find the strength and love,
That keeps me every day.
There are times in our life,
When we lack the courage to keep going on.
But when trouble comes, we must face the task.
Running away is not the answer.

You can't run away from trouble.
There ain't no place that far.
You better find out what road to walk,
If you're gonna be with us at all.
You've got to face it, then you'll make it,
When our problems seem so very hard.
You can't run away from trouble.
There ain't no place that far.
(Repeat)

You got to face it, then you'll make it.
If you believe, you will succeed.
You can't run away from trouble.
There ain't no place that far.

Vocals: Nolanda Smauldon
Backup Vocals: Kurt Bestor, Nolanda Smauldon, and the
  Salt Creek Gospel Choir
Piano: Kurt Bestor

One Note *(Dedicated to Dr. Clynn Barrus)*

Music by Kurt Bestor
Lyrics by Brett Walker
Additional lyrics by Kurt Bestor

Hear, four strings that sing
A bow that flows
Like a ribbon in the wind
Untethered by the man within.
His, a life of work
Now joy made whole
On this perfect violin.

Will, my simple strings
Give voice to sing?
Where's my ribbon in the wind,
A melody within my soul?
Now, can I do as I have heard
On this humble violin.

He said, "I can't play for you,
But only mark the way that I have trod.
No science passes this gift along.
So find your voice unspoken.
Find it from within . . . your song."

Now, with precious time
These strings will sing,
And along will come the wind,
Sweet whisperings from him.
One note.
One joy.

A ribbon in the wind whispers from within,
Come home.

Vocals: Dave Barrus
Solo Violin: Kelly Parkinson
Backup Vocals: Felicia Sorenson
Piano: Kurt Bestor

The Father in Me

Music and lyrics by Nancy Hanson

I can almost see him sittin' here,
For hours he could bend your ear.
A pocket of rocks and a story to go with each.
My grandpa was a simple man,
And with his hands he worked the land.
He loved the earth and all that it had to teach.

And as I think of those wrinkled hands,
Tough as leather, rough as sand,
Old and strong, reaching out to me,
I remember when he taught me how,
To hunt for rocks and work the plow.
He was everything I thought I'd like to be.
Now I'm startin' to see my grandfather in me.

I remember walkin' through the door,
Tools spread all across the floor,
And his legs comin' out from under the kitchen sink.
My daddy was a fix-it man,
Not much he couldn't do with his hands.
He'd let me hold the nail and he'd give my mom a wink.

And as I think of his calloused hands,
Knuckles worn and a wedding band,
Young and strong, reaching out to me,
I remember that he always came,
To my puppet shows and soccer games.
He was everything I thought I'd like to be.
Now I'm startin' to see my father in me.

I fold my hands in thanks for all that I can be.
May this legacy live on inside of me.

And as I'm holdin' these tiny hands,
It's easy now to understand,
My daddy and my grandpa are here with me.
It's in my child's eyes.
And now I realize,
I'm handing down the father in me.

Vocals/Guitar: Nancy Hanson
Piano/Accordian/Synth: Kurt Bestor

A New Father's Prayer

Music by Kurt Bestor
Lyrics by Don Stirling
Additional Lyrics by Kurt Bestor

May these hands learn to lift you,
When the world weighs you down,
And help you stand for truth and right,
When they say it can't be done.
On bended knee I pray—Alleluia and Amen.

May these eyes help you see clearly,
The beauty of a winter's night,
The kiss of spring that brings new life,
Fills the soul with wondrous light.
With bowed head I pray—Alleluia and Amen.

I pray you'll find the treasure
Of a wise and peaceful soul.
I pray you'll never wander,
Wander far from home.

May these ears always listen,
Beyond the words you have to say.
Know the sound of your voice calling,
When you're lost or feel afraid.
Heavenward I pray—Alleluia and Amen.

May this heart be clean and pure,
Forgiving, kind, and true.
A gentle stream that flows,
To your mother and to you.
Humbly I pray—Alleluia and Amen.

Vocals/Synth: Kurt Bestor

Producer: Kurt Bestor
Recording: Dan Carlisle
Assistant Recording Engineer: Corey Cluff
Mix: Barry Gibbons and Dan Carlisle

Recorded at Pinnacle Studios

John McVey appears courtesy of BWE

Violin:	Barbara Williams	Cello:	Ellen Bridger
	Judd Sheranian		Jim Hardy
	Judy Rich		Nicole Jackson
	Katherine Kunz	Oboe:	Holly Gornik
	Kelly Parkinson	Bass:	Ben Henderson
	Lois Swint		James Allyn
	Martha Thompson	French Horn:	Stephen Kostyniak
	Meredith Campbell	Trombone:	Chris Braman
	Natalie Reed	Saxophone:	Ray Smith
Viola:	Christopher McKeller	Drums:	Todd Sorensen
	Joel Rosenberg	Percussion:	Kelly Wallis
	Leslie Harlow	Guitar:	Rich Dixon
	Mario Ortiz	Bass Guitar:	Craig Poole